T0277546

ARS POETICAS

WESLEYAN POETRY

contents

Wesleyan University Press

Middletown CT 06459

www.wesleyan.edu/wespress

© 2025 Juliana Spahr

All rights reserved

Manufactured in Canada

Designed and typeset in Garamond Premier Pro

by Eric M. Brooks

Display photo by Corina Rainer on Unsplash.

Library of Congress Cataloging-in-Publication Data

NAMES: Spahr, Juliana, author.

TITLE: Ars poeticas / Juliana Spahr.

DESCRIPTION: First edition. | Middletown, Connecticut:
    Wesleyan University Press, 2025. | SERIES: Wesleyan poetry |

SUMMARY: "A series of six poems about writing poetry about
    the natural world in a time of both ecological crisis and
    encroaching right-wing populism"— Provided by publisher.

IDENTIFIERS: LCCN 2024031462 (print) | LCCN 2024031463 (ebook) |
    ISBN 9780819501523 (cloth) | ISBN 9780819501530 (ebook)

SUBJECTS: LCGFT: Ecopoetry. | Poetry.

CLASSIFICATION: LCC PS3569.P3356 A88 2025 (print) |
    LCC PS3569.P3356 (ebook) | DDC 811/.54—dc23/eng/20240712

LC record available at https://lccn.loc.gov/2024031462

LC ebook record available at https://lccn.loc.gov/2024031463

5 4 3 2 1

ARS POETICAS

juliana spahr

WESLEYAN UNIVERSITY PRESS

MIDDLETOWN, CONNECTICUT

Ars
Poetica

———— I ————

coral

————————

*The Cold War never
seemed to end and I thought,
"why write poetry; why not
write something useful?"*
INGER CHRISTENSEN

To write poetry after Castle Bravo.
Then to write poetry after 1,500 feet.
After high-quality steel frame buildings,
not completely collapsed, except
all panels and roofs blown in.
After 2,000 feet.
After reinforced concrete buildings collapsed,
or standing but badly damaged.
After 3,500 feet.
After church buildings completely destroyed.
After brick walls severely cracked.
After 4,400 feet.
After 5,300 feet.
After roof tiles bubbled and melted.
After 6,500 feet.
After mass distortion of large steel buildings.
To write the Cold War and doves.
The Cold War and tapeworms.
The Cold War and sails of ships.
The Cold War and the steel of bridges.
To write poetry after that.
To write in a world with few nutrients,
one that rocks back and forth.
The same beginning in both the sea and the land.
To write poetry that knows a hard, cup-shaped skeleton.
And then poetry that knows
the long, stinging tentacles capturing.
Knows the water.
The Atlantic and the Pacific.
The connections between.
The one moving into the other.
To develop poetry in the stomach

that then exits through the mouth
which is the anus.
To write poetry in the blue
that is the absence of green.
Light penetration.
Whorls of tentacles.
The slime earth too.
Hunters and farmers.
Shallow water.
Few nutrients.
High fecundity.
Rapid growth.
Multiarmed morphology and tube feet.
To write tube feet.
To write the exact place.
Seaward slope place.
Sea terrace place.
Algal ridge place.
Coral algal zone place.
Seaward reef flat place.
Islet or interisland reef crest place.
Lagoon reef flat place.
Lagoon terrace place.
Lagoon floor or basin place.
Coral knolls, pinnacle and patch reefs place.
To write poetry after.

scotch
broom

A poem, I thought, I understood, as an
opening, a cracked window maybe, or a

hole in the wall, something I could shimmy through
and then I would be inside a space, ceilings

so high, a lush symphony, elaborate,
filled with movements and all sorts of sounds. I thought

I could fall into the singing, that whoosh. And
so because at first I thought I wanted an

opening in the tautness of tradition,
I glitched this whoosh. I fragmented it into

words or took away its deictics. A poem,
I understood. For years I lived for what was

poetry. I used poetry to shimmy
in, during these years, to build the compounded

patterns of song, even if I recognized
poetry's verses as songs that tend toward

institutional. I thought that poetry
could be apart from the nation still. I thought

that two sorts of poets existed: poets
who write the terrible nation into an

existence and poets fucking around to
do something else. For years I was Team Poets

Fucking Around and Doing Something Else. A
poem, I understood, as a thing read. And

I lived not just for the reading but for that
moment after the reading too. Both the one

where I put down the book and realized I
had been made something other by the words

and the one where I sat in chairs and listened
to the patterns, to the spew of the words that

often had no discernable pattern but
in which I still found meaning floating, sudden,

arriving as the crack of thunder moments
later. I loved the way the abstraction let

me experience my mind clinch and hold tight.
I lived too for when we had to leave the bar

because the poetry reading was over.
Often it was Friday or Saturday night

and the bars were full of the couples who were
willing to pay for the two drink minimums,

so we would keep walking, looking in each bar
and each one wrong. Eventually the streets

would open up and we would be at the bridge
and there would be a river and we would walk

across the open space to it and climb down
its sides and sit. We would have bought some beers and

a small flask of whiskey from a bodega.
We would have carried the cans and the flask in

brown bags as a convention. But we did not
need this convention. If there was law, the law

drove by, didn't stop. Other things were. Night. Maybe
moon. Water. Rats. Sometimes drugs were involved. We

walked through Wall Street at three in the morning once,
rattling the locked doors of all the buildings, then

there laughing at their absurd lights and gilt as
we knew where it was at and it was there at

the rattling of the doors of gilt money. It
was not as if we did not fight. We did. It

was not a paradise, barely a thing that
could be called community. We accepted

too much, were probably too often quick to
accept, seeing things reprehensible as

a sign of the long tradition. A poem,
I understood, as a way to slip away

from the hold of the family, the couple
form, the endless policing of thought, also

everything else that was other than a rich
constant and graceful stretch of openness and

possibility. A road, an exit sign,
a left turn. A poem, I understood, as

words arranged according to some syllabic
convention. Rimbaud's line of eleven count

syllables. And yet Césaire's verrition too.
The poem, I understood, had rules and then

more rules, so many that the result was no
rules mattered that much finally. A poem,

I understood, as a room that could be pried
open by possibility. A room in

Vancouver, early days in the twenty-first
century, where Jeff Derksen said poetry

is a form of atypical thinking, and
I wrote it in a notebook then wrote his

name beside it. I hold on to this still. Oh,
so many poems I understood to be

something divine during these years. There was the
Rukeyser one with the line about the year

the fires would not stop and the world was under
war-shadow. A poem with oranges and

wild cups of silence, the spectacular gift
of revolution. That Shelley poem that

has Hope, that maniac maid, walk out of the fog,
ankle deep in blood, having just slayed all the

assholes. The Whitman one addressed not to
comrades but to the love of comrades. It was

these moments that kept me with poetry a
long time. Since I was a teenager, searching

for meaning. Those loves of many years and our
bodies changing together. A poem, I

understood, as about together, about
how we were together, like it or not. I

used a metaphor of breath and of space. I
embraced all that was epiphanic, used it

to write long poems where each line claimed to be
epiphany, rather than just the end, as

was the lyric convention. I counted the
syllables and filled them with lists of flora

and fauna and called it an elegy. I
joked I had found a sweet spot. I could write a

poem that was too broken for the lyric
poets and too lyric for everyone else.

A poem, I understood. Just as one day
I looked inside a lily, Catalina

Mariposa Lily. One day I said, oh
there is an entire world in the throat, a high-

contrast zone, as they say, and it was so like
walking out into a field at night and there

looking up at stars. I understood I could
not ever write a poem that in any

way had such complexity, variation
as this throat and this galaxy and all that

it held in between, the lizards, mosquitos,
land crabs, the nervous activity of red

ants and cockroaches, muted sky too, bleak
wasteland, swallows flying low. A poem,

I understood, as a theory of the
places I knew, the spirals of the rivers

and brooks, the forests, the woods, the coppices,
the pastures, the towns, and the boroughs. A

poem, I understood, as the fire ants that
latch onto each other and form a living

mound that floats on the water's surface so as
to survive, and also birds that get into

the end of the hurricane's spiral and then
move inward toward the calm until they are

moving with the eye. The theory that makes
up the earth, which is also the theory

of the sea, the theory of the city,
and of the large politics of the state, as

the theory of taking flight. A poem,
I understood, as the moments where I might

be able to think I could possibly so
briefly touch something and yet still bring it to

my throat so as to let it spill out my hand
as a way of atypical thinking. I

knew I used epiphanic lists of flora
and fauna too much to claim them as a way

to make new, and I would try for a while to
stop and then realize that really that

listing was all that mattered to me. I had
so little devotion to a poem, I

understood, as anything other. I had
no desire for a poem that did not at

least stop to notice the soft brown throat of this
Catalina Mariposa Lily and

also the stars and the discourse they shared that
I could not hear and never would be able

to understand, and yet imagining it
was everything that had matter.

When a stick shot across the crowd, it landed at my feet. Then the kid next to me picked it up and ran back into the fight screaming, take this antifa, stick raised over his head. I saw it come down on two heads at the same time. That was all I saw because someone chasing someone else ran between us and they sprayed bear mace, so I looked away, eyes tearing. What I mean here is that it was a time of sticks, not of poems. A time of sticks and a time of a series of street brawls between fa and antifa that sometimes absurdly tumbled into the Berkeley all-organic full-of-strollers farmers market. And also a time of guns, which meant it was also a time when I started to go to the shooting range. There I would be, hands shaking, the gun so heavy, the smell of sulfur in the air, sweeping the cartridges so deep on the floor into the bin at the end. A time, too, when a well-known acquaintance, angry because of unrequited love and wanting to take it out on someone proximate to the one they desired, began posting on facebook about showing up at my office with a gun. A time when friends bought bulletproof vests, a precaution that at first felt absurd to me even though I knew that people had been shot at various street brawls in other cities. Not just a time of street brawls, some won, some lost, but a time when things burned. A time when the fire began to the north and to the south, clustered inland, then spread in both directions, then made it to the sea. A time when there was nothing to do really but watch the fire burn and breathe the smoke that rolled down the street and into the house. A time not just when things burned but when near hurricane level winds carried the fire across highway 1. A time when there were no longer any air purifiers for sale because the smoke was everywhere. So a time too of supply-chain collapse. And a time of social intensity. A time when the DMs and the @s came in from all different directions, so fast and furious it was as if they were a franchise. *The Fast and the Furious* that was about the editor. Then *2 Fast 2 Furious* about the managing editor, followed by the time when *The Fast and the Furious:*

Tokyo Drift was about myself, and then the time when I initiated *Fast &*
Furious, which was about you. A time when I wanted to say I'm sorry, by
which I mean sorry that I took your work so seriously that I thought it
mattered, sorry for working out my own heart that hurts all over your
work, sorry also for feeling terrible when someone else did the same to
me. A time when I felt I had to call my mom and tell her that her name
was on 4chan under a post that began, "Here are a bunch of commie jew
faggots." A time when I then had to explain that she was not the commie
jew faggot, it was because she had birthed me. A time too when 4chan's
anonymity was not really the default because the brawlers were no longer
afraid to show their faces and had activated an instagram account where
they shared their t-shirt designs, their Nordic tattoos, their gym-begotten
muscles. A time when a white nationalist began posting pictures of his
arsenal in South Africa and saying he was coming for my family. So again
and again, a time of guns. A time full of days when there was no sun, the
smoke so thick. It was a time of demands for apologies and a time of
refusals to accept the apologies that were offered in response to the
demand. A time when I began to learn the rhythms, how it peaks around
forty-eight hours, then it's all over, a friend jokes, when Tucker finally
tweets about it. A time when I often gave up, waited for Tucker to tweet,
as it were. A time when I could no longer tell what was comedy, what was
farce, what was merely a meme. A time when one day in Berkeley, a day
of many brawls at the farmers market, a dumpster was pushed back and
forth, an antifa shove followed by an Oath Keeper shove followed by
an antifa shove followed by an Identity Evropa shove. A time when
everything, even a meme, seemed like it could turn more serious. And
a time when, though I knew about the terribleness of 4chan trolls, I
knew they were likely irrelevant combined with the double bind of also
knowing that there were moments in history when considering Nazis
irrelevant didn't go well at all. A time of days when there was no sun,
only red haze so thick. And yet not a time in which I was important or
mattered. A time when there is no denying I got the least of it; no one in
the legislature tried to pass a law that I should be fired. And I don't mean
to imply it was all bad. A time of oh, those nights when the fight felt vital

and all was not yet lost. A time when so many dance parties played one of the many versions of "Fuck tha Police" that are available in this time and the costumed seethed together in a shared hatred of fascism and I joined in, awkwardly seething too. A time of these moments of triumph, oh so fleeting, oh so trivial in the face of the daily. A time when there were avatars on twitter who acted as if they knew, who would sometimes lecture-tweet: those of you who don't notice how fascism arrives, I can assure you it isn't on cat's feet. A time, thus, when avatars on twitter assumed most had not read the history, that most had never felt the sharpness of a cat's claws. But it was a time when I cohabitated with cats, so it wasn't that I didn't notice. I did. I understood. Because it was a time when I read history books. But also a time when there was little that a poem, I understood. A time when I could not figure out how to write that epiphanic line of possibility. A time when it was never clear what to do, poetry or otherwise. A time when some gathered their children close and decided to wait it out. A time when others photographed the day with no sun and posted it on their socials. Still others left the consciousness of earth. Some of these others momentarily, through powders and pills. Too many of them left permanently. A time when I asked one who came back from death what it was like over there and he said nothing; it is nothing; there is nothing on the other side. And I couldn't help thinking: just like a poem, another sort of nothing. So a poem, I understood, had no room for this life in this moment. A time when the nights with the fights felt vital. A time when I would say, I am lost, and they would say, come down to the plaza. I would say ok and suit up, by which I mean I would put on my jeans and my running shoes and my many layers of flannel and stick a water bottle in my bag. Then I would meet them there in the late afternoon light. Often it was winter, so it would be dark soon. Sometimes it was summer with hours of light still. I would mill around, listen to others declaim, perhaps nodding my head at those I recognized, maintaining that decades-old convention of detached cool. Last week was a time when dark came early, and suddenly the moms were getting teargassed, despite their big red heart-shaped signs designed to say don't hit me; I'm a mom; I craft. A time when some sort of feds, I didn't even know who they were, were disappearing people. A time when I learned the term "show of force" was also a helicopter maneuver. A time when even though I knew to show the fuck up I couldn't or didn't or was too tired. And then there was the rest of life. A time when I went to little league games as often as I talked about revolution. More often than I talked about poetry. Like the song of summer, the foul ball always came out of nowhere. And all the kids each time ran for it. This would happen multiple times each game. I've got it. I've got it. They all would yell this. I've got it. Rarely did anyone have it. Sometimes I wore my Sappho hat, and at other times I wore the one that says HOWL to these games. I refused the one that says Spicer, but that's another story. In the hours before dusk the light is luminous and I recognized it at the time as the poem of the breeze. A time when the song of the summer was the one about Old Town Road. I hated it at first and then I loved it.

I'm concerned about these other things. Or that is what I thought
when they said they were worried I no longer understood the poem, the
poetry. It was summer. Still afternoon. We had half a day of this beauty
before us and we knew it. Unhurried. Pleasure. We drank a beer that
was fresh on the tongue in a new way. Light. Almost carbonated. In the
afternoon sun, the breeze blew softly. The sky was blue. I first protested to
them not about poetry but about the structural condition of poets, the
required courting of institutional authority, the lucky with their listings
of grants and prizes won, the resentments of those less lucky fighting for
attention on facebook or twitter. The troubles that define this moment:
#somanypoems and #sofewreaders and #whatreadersexistareallpoetstoo
plus #suchalongtradition. One thought I had as we talked was love
the poem but hate being the poet, hate this frayed cloth called poetry
community. I mean, there have always been poets and always poets
writing a terrible sociality into someone's inbox, but there is so much
going to the inbox right now. But what I said to them was something
much more mundane. They write rengas to Obama, I said. As if that
was something so obviously onerous that I didn't even have to explain it.
They laughed, shrugged as if to say that clearly there are so many worse
things one can do with one's time, and show up with sticks to fight at
the Berkeley all-organic farmers market is one of them. But what they
actually said was it has never not been a terrible nation, and there have
always been poets too, always poets willingly writing the terrible nation
into existence; there is nothing new to this moment. Still, I thought, this
latest round where poets were writing rengas to Obama is one reason
a poem, I no longer understood. They were right; poetry and me, our
relationship was tenuous. They recognized that I couldn't write the
singing or the not singing. So I said to them, I'm not concerned that a
poem, I no longer understand. They were generous to notice, to care,
but still a frayed relationship to poetry is an almost universal condition.

I mean, so many poems are about the not liking of poetry, and here I am writing another one. Still, it would be too easy to blame my failing relationship with poetry on poetry itself. Or that is what I told them that afternoon. I knew what poetry was, what it stood for, when I first started putting words into patterns and calling it a poem. Instead, I said, I'm concerned about these other things. This nation, our nation. How it was first something terrible and now something possibly more terrible. So even while a poem, I understood, could be about righteous anger or revolutionary love or hatred of nation or hatred of fascism, I couldn't hear this singing. Dark times. And poetry with its hopes and joys just felt silly. Even the poems I once understood, loved. And it all felt like a loss, losing this terrible nation to something more terrible and losing the way I had once put words together and dedicated them to the love of comrades. But still, even while a poem, I no longer understood, I would wake up and my head would hurt, and then I would realize that in my dream I had said to myself that I should write some poetry. But my dreams never explained to me why. Or how, never explained how to sing in these dark times. One thing I've noticed is that those who never bother to read poetry are the most convinced the world would be less without it, as they mistake its irrelevance as a form of resistance. A friend dropped by on her way to the doctor to get a ketamine push. A nurse was going to push the dose incrementally and take her into a hole for an hour. Before she left, I asked her if she could please, when she was in the hole, at least ask or wonder why there was poetry. She texted me hours later: orange and yellow; the breeze off the bay. She meant that same breeze I had days ago been enjoying with beers. She added: the clouds; Mount Diablo in the distance; the warm sun. Then a few days later she texted: there needs to be some pleasure in the world. And, a few minutes later: poetry is what is left of life; more singing. I texted back Brecht: in the dark times; will there also be singing?; yes, there will also be singing; about the dark times. I had begun to read Brecht at night, in bed with my son while he too read before he went to sleep. I was reluctant, imageless, lost a little too, not in the middle of the words but in the middle of all that defines this world, this moment, a busy street corner might be the only way to think of it.

A poem, I understood, to be a place for the questions, not for the answers. I picked up Brecht to understand how to write all the peace and the war, the order and the chaos, the joy and the despair at the same time. What is a poem, I told myself, if not that magical thing that inventories everything so that the harms and hurts of all our lives are understood in some way. I thought if I just read all of Brecht, I would maybe find the singing. There was a new edition. It was hard to hold because it was so big. I rested it on a pillow, and I rested my head on a pillow, and I turned the pages looking for the singing. I couldn't find the singing. What I found instead were a series of questions. Brecht did not answer. Turned to Rukeyser. Also did not answer. I thought briefly of that shield made for Achilles. The one where the moon and the sun shine at the same time. The one with the two cities, with the sowing and the reaping. The one that ends with the ocean. And then I went back to twitter and watched a video of the feds that are more or less a militia right now arrest an old man who brought a leaf blower to a protest so as to blow back the endless teargas.

That day as the breeze blew and the beer we drank
was vibrant, bubbly, and we were delighted

with it, I said, I love Césaire. I said this to
them in that late afternoon light, the sort that

throws its patterns on the walls. I love Césaire, I
said, because he had neither facebook nor

twitter. And then added Shelley. Césaire, Shelley,
Rukeyser I mumbled later, as we walked home.

Brecht, Fodeba Keïta, Blake. Oh, Rimbaud also,
of course. What I didn't tell them was that in the

car, driving home the other night, I listened
to an old friend read on the other side of

the continent. I listened on my phone, which
was hooked into the car stereo. The road, it

twisted and turned. The moon overhead, a sort
of red and also a yellow. Poems full

of debts to the troubadours filled the car's small
space. When they worked, it was a hubris gone right.

And who doesn't love a gamble? But that was not
what struck me. What I loved about this thing I

knew, occasional poem, was how it might
hold the moment, just the moment, nothing more.

Like that Creeley poem. The one that has a
car in it and someone is driving, someone

in the car is called John but that is not his
name. The driver who doesn't seem to be a good

driver, because then someone such as John who
is not exclaims, "for / christ's sake, look / out where yr

going." Or I liked to think I could be John
who is not the driver, but still I hold this

warning even though the poet there always just
talking, always just to say that the darkness

surrounds us and what can we do against it
or else why not buy a goddamn big car. But

once one finds oneself in that car, look out where
it is going. These lines made some whole, some hole

in the fabric of this thing that is called a
poem but is just arranged words. After I

started reading Brecht, I began sorting through
my books. I had too many. As I pulled them

off the shelves, blew off the dust, I asked myself
would I need it in a revolution? It

turned out that I thought I would for sure need five
translations of the Odyssey and all the

books of Susan Howe. I kept all the plant books
too. The comfort of the *Jepsen Manual*

of Vascular Plants of California.
It's an open question if that possible

revolution will still need poetry, its
tradition and its resistance to that tradition, but

it will for sure need the *Vascular Plants of
California.* Here is the thing, all these

terrible things happen and still one gets up
in the morning and with one's ears, unbidden,

the trill of a small bird enters, and with that
trill the ear tells the brain to hold delight and

all is fine, all will be fine too. Same with the
laughter of the children in the park next to

the bedroom window. The trill and the laughter,
these things go on, despite. Despite the fa and

antifa fighting in the streets. Despite the
latest stock market crash. Despite these endless

cataclysmic collapses of this beauty.
All that is happening. Despite today the

Gulf Stream seems to be slowing because a cold
blob is developing off of Greenland. All

this and more. Despite whatever there is that
is terrible in this day, there is still the

trill, the laughter, the poem that builds around
the moon which has a cloud over it and is

so beautiful. So so powerful all this
all will be fine when really everything

is terrible and really the part of
us that loves moon, poetry, trill, laughter is

the same part of what is ever so wrong with
us. As despite the pleasure nothing is changed,

all is still terrible. How many ways do
we know it? I would say a lot. A friend is

dying as the scotch broom is putting out its
nitrogen-fixing roots but our hard and long

friendship died years before the seed pods all burst
open explosively spread yet one more friend

has cancer and other things and they last for
eighty years and yet another friend now in

the world in some new way but they are hard and
survive rough transport through water and mainly

it was all the information fleshy and
full of proteins in a way that interests

ants we suddenly knew about everything
as the ants carry the seeds back to their nests

creating dense infestations. A mixture
of hell. A metaphor of resilience.

The scotch broom has many
tricks. Grows in patches and also scattered with

total cover of about fifteen percent
and thirty-five percent, respectively. As

does the Tree of Heaven. There is no space too
polluted for it as it absorbs sulfur

dioxide in its leaves. It can withstand cement
dust and fumes from coal tar operations

as well as resist ozone exposure. And
even mercury too. It grows fast, even

faster in California. And yet once
it starts, it shows up everywhere, as it is

impossible to destroy. Loves fires. And is
fine. Everything. Never ending. Everything.

Yet to come. Yellow veins. Flowers. Large, compound
leaves. Arranged. Alternately on the stem. Then

eleven to thirty-three leaflets. Sometimes
up to forty-one. One to three teeth on each

side. Close to the base. Everything. Small. Yellow-
green to reddish. Flowers. Everything. Clusters

of flowers up to thirty centimeters
long. Everything. My hope is that in the near

future all my worry looks foolish and wrong.
I hope there was no need to be so distraught

about poetry, especially when it
has put up with me for so long and also

generously given me so much to read,
and some of it actually great. For it

is despite the fires that never seem to end,
the world and leaves continue to exist and

someone has to notice. And also is
it really that wrong to have a few short

moments where we breathe and say it will be fine,
we will make it through in some form while it all

burns? In the rest of life there will be singing
for sure but the choice might be less obvious

than I realize. So yes, there will be song
in the end times. But is it the end times? All

signs point to yes but the end times, I vision
them dramatic, full of pestilence and blood,

yet in this moment there is no hint of a
thing like revolution. By the time the state

was burning from both ends and one end went by
the name Paradise, I didn't bother with the

metaphor. Instead I just noticed the smoke,
shut the window, stayed indoors, and kept right on

typing. Later I joked, now I know what I
will be doing when the world burns; I will be

shutting the windows and catching up on my
email finally. I didn't joke about writing

a poem. Probably a sign they matter
still. The fire was much, and I knew I was small

before it, and there was more to come. The year
whose fires would not stop, Rukeyser wrote, a year

held by a wild cup of silence.

bluebird-
ghost

Warblers and the northeast-flowing
winds ride together down
the river these cool spring
nights. Sugar maples, beech,
and northern red oaks grow
to a largeness, helped by
ferns and fungi. The bobcat and
the woodrat shelter beneath. Nearby,
the Virginia creeper and its leaves of
five adhesive tips, its carefree
ball-like fruits, twine around
the sawbriers that grow so
fast overnight that it is as   .
if by the foot. The familiar bluet
hovers over, above, around.
As you well know, this
place is weighty, tawdry, the soil
redolent, the symphony terrestrial.
The sun's late-day glimmer
pleases so much it might as
well be fireworks. A
choreography of eddies and
currents fed by tributaries — the
Muskingum, the Miami, the
Wabash, and the Scioto from
the south; the Tennessee, the
Big Sandy, and the Licking
from the north — that babble happily. You
add a siren off in the distance, pause
dramatically to list the names of
everyone you once kissed beneath
its bridges in the darkness that

harmonizes with fecundity. And
then you, never one to hold
back, insist on putting just one
more bird on it, if only because
you want to dwell with the
words golden-winged, chestnut-
sided, and yellow-rumped. That
feeling of possibility, that you can
hold both of the river's climates, the
subtropical one and the continental
one, in a few lines. That conviction that
all it takes is to find a few words in
the dictionary, inventory a dangerous
lexicon of allure, and allow a fleeting
encore to come out the other side.
That belief that a poem can meaningfully
insist that someone take a moment and
just bother with beauty, that someone
will understand a poem to be an
intricate sonnet of interconnected streams,
that someone will claim there
is a political beauty in a few important-
sounding words arranged in rough
syllable counts. By someone you
mean a clown, curly red hair, exaggerated
red and white lips, something funny
going on with the eyebrows, the
sort that suddenly shows up in this
locale, celebrating the intrinsic beauty
of this space with yet another poem
about lost opportunity and bad timing
in relationships. By clown you mean
yourself just moments ago. All of
that gone. You can't say it that way

anymore. No one can. A dog is
barking as you turn your head to
see the coal barge floating down the
river's curves, heading to the power
plant off in the near distance,
ominous beneath the blue plume of
smoke produced by its smokestacks.
Horace makes fun of those who
write of babbling brooks. And he did not
even know about coal barges and
capitalism, much less the
late capitalism that blossomed while
you sat around thinking about
the cuteness of a bobcat and a
woodrat, two enemies, sheltering
under a very large sugar maple in
an image of an impossible pax
Americana. If only for the sake
of self-analysis, you think something
ought to be written about the cooling
towers, the 765-kilovolt transmission
lines, the smokestacks, the blue
plume that regularly dusts the tubal
inflorescences of the bee balm, the
stubby blue flowers of the wild
indigo, the polished, vibrant red,
deeply five-lobed racemes of the
pinnately cut and lobed wood poppy,
and the dark green and the black of
the white wood aster. Even that
bobcat and that woodrat sheltering
beneath get plumed. Years ago
because of the plume everyone
human in town packed up their

houses and left, pocketing three
times the market value for them.
Bee balm, blue indigo, wood
poppy, white wood aster, bobcat,
woodrat obviously had nothing
to sell and so settled
in, tolerating. Horace suggests
couplets and iambs to
tell a tragic tale, this tragic tale of
particles, sulfates, and nitrates, water,
gaseous nitrogen dioxide, sulfur trioxide,
full of mercury, of polyfluorinated
alkyl substances of emissions, coal ash fly,
humid bottom ash, boiler slag, scrubber sludge of
fluidized bed combustion ash, residues, milky
drops soot and white specks, all carried by southern winds.
. There you go again,
counting syllables as your index
fingers drum out an elusive beat
on your wooden desktop. You never
wanted to lose faith in a poem, the
many intricate interplays between
love, the natural world, and statements
of identity. That elusive calculus of
seventy, twenty, and ten percent
that defies neat delineation.
But it was not like you ever
bothered to have faith in it,
even as you rhymed
sulfates and nitrates. After
the barge passes by, a
picnic on the car's hood ensues.
Cheese, crackers, and onion are
consumed in a liminal space. You

have to do this sometimes, come
out into the open. It is some
puzzle, how you continue
standing here as if to sing while
breathing the smoke of the pit,
the air saturated, the river's
steeped history, as birds peck
away at fellow birds. And yet
what else are you doing here
besides hoping to find some
sort of instruction manual on
how to refrain this song,
where elk graze beside the strong
oak tree, hunted down, yet
persisting, a song, akin to night
heron-ghost and bluebird-ghost,
stuttering to each other,
if only for the desire to
communicate. Comforting
is a complicated word.

bison

Right at the beginning of art: the bison.
There it is on the walls of various caves,
cavorting with the horses and the ibexes.
At moments, bison pauses
mid-frolic tail raised.
Sometimes bison is shockingly red.
Always beautiful.
Always full of life, even when dying.
Is this not an art of what matters?
What comes after that is something else.
By which I mean all that art about the hunt
that comes from the European eye.
Currier and Ives, *Life on the Prairie: The Buffalo Hunt*, 1862,
    followed by after Arthur Boyd Houghton, *Buffalo Hunting:*
    A Jamboree, 1871, followed by after Arthur Boyd Houghton, *Buffalo*
    Hunting: In Search of Buffalo and Coming to Grief, 1871, followed
    by after Arthur Boyd Houghton, *Buffalo Hunting — Camping Out,*
    1871, followed by Theodore Baur, *The Buffalo Hunt*, 1876, followed
    by Charles M. Russell, *Buffalo Hunt*, 1905, followed by *Hunting the*
    Buffalo from Fry & Sons Hunting Series, 1918.
And that is just what the Met owns.
They don't even have a cast of
Frederic Remington's 1907
The Buffalo Horse,
the one that supposedly represents
the unsettled west
but really represents
a bison that was living
in a zoo in the Bronx.

The reasons why there are thousands of representations
of buffalo hunts in state museums
and none of a bison on its back making the wallow
probably have to do with how Buffalo Bill Cody killed
over four thousand bison in eighteen months.
He shot sixty-eight in an eight-hour period.
The railroad and the gun.
There is human ingenuity again, failing us.
And here is human ingenuity
trying to pick up the pieces,
hundreds of years later.
Still, that Remington.
It is hard not to think there is art again, failing us.

When the bison wallows,
it is not just that the dust rises up.
The soil compacts, hair and oil mix in it,
eventually there is a deep impression,
one that fills with water when the rains come.
Then an impossible art results,
the bison way of making things right
for the feathery leaves of the yarrow,
the purple- or pink-tinted stalks of the field milk vetch,
the stalkless flowers of the cushion phlox,
and the wispy pink plumes of the prairie smoke.
Tall bluebells too, pendant bell-shaped,
next to the simple yellow flowers of the alpine arnica.
The bison way of making things right
for the wooly gray leaves of the fringed sage,
right too for the sage's small and unremarkable fruits.
Right for the roots of the Jerusalem artichokes,
the prairie turnip and the prairie parsley.
Right for the prairie chicken.
The bison way of making things right for the male
to come hooting, dancing, tail up,
neck sacks inflated all the while.
Right for the western chorus frogs
that come out at night to chorus and feed.
Right for the high jumping northern cricket frog.
Right for the small invertebrates and arthropods
upon which they feed. The sap-feeding herbivores
with their beak mouthpart sucking on plant fluid.
The chewing herbivores with their
mandibulate mouthparts. And those that

carnivorously feed on a variety of prey.
Right also for the grasshopper sparrow, also feeding,
and then creating a well-concealed open cup
on the ground under the tall stalks of the big bluestem,
the shorter ones of the little bluestem,
the switchgrass and the Indiangrass too.

There was once a prairie.
It's never coming back,
as in it will never be whole again.
There's the bison.
They can come back.
But the bison plus the prairie,
as in the bison moving over the prairie
with the rumored speed of a race horse,
that too is never coming back
until we change the well-intentioned
hopes of institutions of research,
the less well-intentioned grants
for rewilding from banks and governments,
into something psychotic and large
in its demands,
by which I mean the end of capitalism.
Really, I don't want to land this poem so hard,
land it on a word so clichéd as "capitalism,"
but I don't know how to say otherwise
about this predicament we are in
where there is only one way out.
That it's an idea that feels impossible
to include in a poem tells us something
about the new feats of imagining we
have yet to embrace.

goby

Here, floating with the water
I escape. I float. I immerse in the richness
of the forest; fade into the dark greens
of the ferns and reeds of the shore,
the light greens of the new leaves on the trees,
the water rushing, and oh the bird calls too.
Came to sedate, cleanse, escape.
Came to clear out my dreams
filled with bears that each night enter
my room, tearing it apart
so as to let me know there aren't enough
fish this year and likely the next too.
Came for water so clear
that I could wash, that I could see.
Came to see a goby,
a blue, a purple, a turquoise
too when seen from the side,
then a clear that is as a pink when it turns.

Even as it is getting dark so fast
that there is almost nothing left to see
still, we together swim on, into some world
not yet imagined, not yet understood.
Oh goby, I am sorry we have made things
so impossible for you, for all of us.
Sorry that we have done so much that
you are few; sorry to be so lost, imageless,
confused; sorry that I do not know how to be
other than Grendel, swamp-like, dwelling in fen
and moorland, up to my knees in the water,
wandering the outskirts of town, angry,
unforgiving of those who still find happiness
amidst such gut-wrenching loss.
Goby, even the very things
that would cure us we put at risk:
the tall tapering racemes of white midsummer
flowers on wiry black-purple stems
that are the black cohosh; the blood-red sap
of the bloodroot and its small white petals that
open up in sunlight; the hairy deep purple
stems of the goldenseal that support
two hand-shaped leaves.
This world that once was so much, now less.
This world that was once a luminous archive
of things evolved and adapted in slow-moving
specificity. This world that Césaire wrote
when there was the possibility
that it might turn some other way than the nation,
a world not of enclosure but of predatory

celebration, liberation, a world of the sparrowhawk,
the cynocephalus, the dolphins, and the wolves
who feed in the untamed openings.
Fled is that music, that world, that rhetorical question.
We continue on, angry, unforgiving, unsure.

coral,
again

And the big, long waves surge
through the interreef passages
and break on the outermost reefs.
There a sea-foam is made
from the strong hydrodynamic forces.
A witness of sorts to tidal flows, surf zones,
these powerful turbulent jets and eddies
around the flanks of reef.
Beneath the whiteness,
the coral on the shallow bottom
rests its cells in the dappled sunlight.
And there also the single-celled algae.
Two forms of energy and capture these two,
as a lover and a beloved in a lyric.
When the waves are low there is sunlight
and so the holobiont is happy, growing.
When the water is turbid, when the light is limited,
the corals then eat the algae.
This too a form of happy.
By eating I mean the algae lives inside
the digestive cavity of the coral.
By happy I mean the give and take of
vitamins, trace elements, nutrients, carbon dioxide
that should be understood as the most primal of loves.
The lesson here is one of living in or on one another
so as to build, maintain, and defend.
One could make a politics of it.
That is what confused Ovid did.
Misunderstanding the coral as stone,
not understanding its life.
In his telling, Perseus created it when he

nestled Medusa's head in plants
he found below the waves.
This was right after he slayed the sea monster
so as to win Andromeda.
Andromeda, she too was something else,
something impossible for him to recognize.
For she is lapped by sea-foam, as the Loeb puts it.
Meaning she was of this intertidal realm,
of the coral and the algae.
When Perseus arrives he pulls her out and away.
And what follows is the supposed
first representation of a man falling in love
with a woman on a stage.
No one ever says anything about
Andromeda falling in love.
And of course, why would they?
Andromeda seems rather aware
that her options are limited to slave or wife or servant.
Is it not all here, in a story retold so many times?
Is it not all we need to know about how hard
it is for us to go forward?
And also all the ways possible?
Beneath the foam is all the symbiosis
that a Bakuninist could want.
A poet too; all the metaphor a poet could want.
All the choices for imagining survival
as living in or on one another
in the coral-rich intertidal zone
of Andromeda,
fish flickering in and out,
the big, long waves surging
through the interreef passages
to break on the outermost reef where

a sea-foam is made
from the strong hydrodynamic forces.
There, a witness too.
Tidal flows, surf zones, the flanks of reef.

ARS
POETICA
——— 7

acknowledgments

I like to think of myself as someone who goes it alone, at the back of the room, sunglasses on, expressionless.

Sunglasses on, expressionless. In 1986 I was at a Black Flag concert in Poughkeepsie, and I overheard someone describe me as impossible to talk to and always alone in my room writing poetry. I felt anointed; it was as if I had finally made it out of Chillicothe.

Out of Chillicothe. There was a possibility that I could remake myself as someone independent of the heavy debts of family and farm town and something as close to poverty as to working class.

To working class. Right after this, someone threw a cookie on the stage and Henry Rollins picked it up and rubbed it all over his sweaty body, in between his ass crack, and then ate it.

And ate it. This is the show where Greg Ginn's guitar was stolen and he just went and got another one and didn't care, or so the story goes.

The story goes that Greg Ginn too had a version of going it alone where even the guitar didn't matter.

Guitar didn't matter. Later that night my friend got detained for drawing cartoons with a sharpie on the bathroom tile. He was drunk or high; I don't remember which. I talked him out of the back of the police car.

The police car. I never go it alone. I'm not sure anyone can. That's my point.

That's my point. There are always friends and police.

Friends and police. I wrote all the poems in this book because someone asked.

Because someone asked, usually via email. A version of "Ars Poetica 1" first appeared in *Trappe Tusind*, written after Nanna Søndergaard Larsen asked for work that celebrated Inger Christensen.

Celebrated Inger Christensen. Most of what is now "Ars Poetica 2" was written at first because of talking with Syd Staiti and also because Andrea Abi-Karam and Kay Gabriel asked me to read at Segue. A section of this poem appeared in *Action, Spectacle* thanks to Joshua Clover and Adam Day. An excerpt of an earlier version appeared in the catalog for a show called *Illiberal Arts* at Haus der Kulturen der Welt, after Anselm Franke and Kerstin Stakemeier asked. A different version appeared under the title "Will There Be Singing" for Poem-a-Day thanks to Ari Banias. And another part appeared in *Lana Turner* because David Lau and Cal Bedient asked for "poems responding to the year 2017," the year of the Battles for Berkeley.

Battles for Berkeley. Angie Sijun Lou asked me to write a poem for *Dark Soil*, a collection of works inspired by Karen Tei Yamashita. I wrote a poem about Cheshire, Ohio, a town that barely exists anymore, as American Electric Power bought most of the houses after residents complained about health issues from the coal burning. But when I tried to bring that poem into this book, the balance of it felt all wrong. What is now "Ars Poetica 3" is about writing that poem.

Writing that poem. A version of "Ars Poetica 4" was written for *Creature Conserve: Writing at the Intersection of Art and Science* after Christopher Kondrich asked for poems about the uncertain fate of the animal world for an anthology featuring a range of species from bees and bats to eels and bison.

Eels and bison. "Ars Poetica 5" appeared in Poem-a-Day thanks to Claudia Rankine. All she asked for were some poems. There was no mandate.

Was no mandate. A version of "Ars Poetica 6" was to appear in *Something On Paper*, although it is unclear to me if it will ever appear, but, still, I wrote it thanks to Bill Shultz, who asked for work on "Imagining Survival, Reckoning with Extinction: Poetics and Politics in the Capitalocene."

In the capitalocene and merely dialogue and occasional, these poems make no claims to be epic's song filled with Beowulf's alliterative anger and strength. Not a glimpse of power.

Glimpse of power. Not the more contemporary version of this epic, loud with righteous anger about wrongs the poet has experienced. Not shamanic invocations either.

Shamanic invocations either. Obviously also not the lyrics of those still young, full of ohs and elaborate beauties cloaked in metaphors that preen and delight.

Preen and delight. I don't know what these poems are other than patterned language that is requested, and thus occasional, thus dialogue. Possibly, a danse macabre of ecological grief perhaps.

Ecological grief perhaps.

My ecological grief perhaps. I have never figured out how to move from grief to call to action. But then I'm convinced poetry is not a call to action. Or not a good one.

A good one. I mean there are all sorts of poems and if I had to say the sort of poem that hits me hard, makes me go oh the most often, it is the sort that first says everything is fucked because all these beautiful things will be gone, which then allows the inventory of the beautiful things that will soon be gone to swell into the heart.

Into my heart. I seem to think of poetry as that moment when all gets still right before the terrible. Perhaps. On days when I want to give it all up, tired of its invocations and laments, I remind myself Grendel came to town to get his revenge. It for sure didn't go well. For his troubles he first got his arm torn off, and then he got his head cut off, and then there was much rejoicing. But there he is in the poem, and with him comes everything fen and moorland, mists, marshes, inaccessible lands, cold-flowing currents, all that steams and bubbles, and even the bottom of the sea with its monsters. And right after him comes John Clare, also of fen and moorland and yet a poet.

Yet a poet. The enclosure is such a metaphor of all that is terrible; that Clare poem about the dead little mouldywharps hanging off the fences that enclose the moors and in a silent murmuring complains.

Silent murmuring complains. This long tradition of poetry of ecological collapse, and here we are still looking at things that are beautiful in patterned language. Or I cannot resist such beauty. I set out to write about the coal barges, and the poem becomes about the beauty of the river. Is there any way to write something other than the danse macabre, is it possible to write not a dance on a grave but an inventory of care, that luminous archive that Césaire invokes, a path of wormy meandering?

Of wormy meandering. Still, because I am anxious about the large claim, I wanted to ask Christopher Kondrich to take the bison away and give me something smaller to write about. I would have been happy with the bdelloid rotifer, the one that came back to life after being frozen for 24,000 years and the first thing it did was reproduce asexually. Next it ate, I suspect.

Ate, I suspect. That's a poem, no? Tradition held in suspended animation only to be reactivated in the lab, reproducing, consuming, reproducing again, changing a little each time but holding fast to the measured form. Frozen, and the ice an archive.

Ice an archive, but god what a fucking mess. The bdelloid rotifer had been frozen in Siberia for over 24,000 years and was in the lab because the tundra melts as I write these lines.

Write these lines, for poetry is less something frozen come back to life, multiplying and ingesting, egalitarian perhaps, and more something that is ivy-covered, expensive, a reminder of some of the things I can't take about the European tradition.

The European tradition, and yet those lines about how poetry is a sort of bread or that one about how it is not a luxury. Perhaps those things are true, but we have treated poetry as if it is not bread, have wrapped it in tissue paper and stuck it in a bag with other luxury goods. To get it back will take a dismantling of everything around it.

Everything around it. So many claims made about a genre that is defined perhaps most obviously by the shortness of its lines.

Of its lines. Such a modest genre. Still, the European tradition or the wallow. When I gave in to the bison, I realized I could do worse than think of the poem as the dirt the bison kicks up.

Bison kicks up.

Bison kicks up. Still, I find my metaphor more in water. I have always been a sponge, the sort of sea sponge that exists only by the grace of water flowing constantly through my body, except water here is the words of others, which means all words.

Means all the words. The descriptions of coral in "Ars Poetica 1" and "Ars Poetica 6" both came from the *Encyclopedia of Modern Coral Reefs*, edited by David Hopley, from the chapter on "Bikini Atoll, Marshall Islands."

Means all the words. The first line of John Ashbery's "And *Ut Pictura Poesis* Is Her Name" is "You can't say it that way anymore." It is the sixty-sixth and -seventh lines of "Ars Poetica 3."

Means all the words. Jason Eric Baldes's "Cultural Plant Biodiversity in Relict Wallow-like Depressions on the Wind River Indian Reservation, Wyoming, and Tribal Bison Restoration and Policy" — especially table 3.2, a list of the species of plants found in wallow-like depressions — shaped "Ars Poetica 4." It was also written in response to "Challenges and Opportunities for Cross-jurisdictional Bison Conservation in North America," an article Christoper Kondrich asked me to read by Liba Pejchar, Lissett Medrano, Rebecca M. Niemiec, Jennifer P. Barfield, Ana Davidson, and Cynthia Hartway.

Means all the words. None of you consented, and yet I took.

Yet I took, Andrea Abi-Karam, John Ashbery, Jason Eric Baldes, Jennifer P. Barfield, Anselm Franke, Kay Gabriel, David Hopley, Christopher Kondrich, Nanna Søndergaard Larsen, Lissett Medrano, Angie Sijun Lou, Rebecca M. Niemic, Liba Pejchar, Claudia Rankine, Edmund Selous, Bill Shultz, Kerstin Stakemeier, Syd Staiti. I took and took. Still I'm sorry for all the ways these have failed.

These have failed and all the things I've said wrong.

Have said wrong and for taking too, all the debts I have overlooked.

I have overlooked and so many thefts, but nonetheless it was generous for some of you to have a faith in poetry and generous to ask me too to have a faith.

Have a faith, a momentary suspension of disbelief.

Suspension of disbelief. Sorry too to anyone who ended up in this poem and doesn't want to be here.

To be here.

To be here, with my failure that defines these poems; a failure, I'm sure you know, that is not your failure.

Not your failure, the natural world. Earlier today I bent down to tie my shoe and there were the smallest of flowers, so small I had not noticed them, but then once my eyes adjusted I saw them everywhere.

Saw them everywhere. They were everywhere, as one might say about poetry.

Say about poetry.

Say about poetry, do you know: is it that smallest of flowers, invisible until there it is as far as the eye can see? Or my shoe, clumsily almost crushing that flower?

Crushing that flower.

END

about the author

JULIANA SPAHR is a writer and scholar of literature. Her most recent book of poetry, *That Winter the Wolf Came*, takes as its concern the global spread of political struggles located at the intersection of ecological and economic catastrophe. She also publishes literary prose. Highly fictionalized but still probably memoir, *Army of Lovers* was cowritten with David Buuck and tells the story of two mediocre poets who are attempting to write poetry in a time when poetry's importance is on the decline. Her most recent book of scholarship, *Du Bois's Telegram: Literary Resistance and State Containment*, explores the ambiguous and disconcerting role that literature plays in upholding the modern nation-state. She was also the editor, with Claudia Rankine, of *American Women Poets in the 21st Century*. https://www.weslpress.org/readers-companions/